The History of

The Church and Parish of ST. ANDREW OXMARKET CHICHESTER

by

Alison McCann

Assistant Archivist

ISBN 0 0900801 41 7

Published by West Sussex Record Office
John Edes House
Chichester

W S C C

1978

The Font, 1852

The present building of the church of St. Andrew Oxmarket was erected in the thirteenth century. Since the earliest documentary reference to the church dates from 1248, it would seem reasonable to assume that the original foundation of the church and parish was in the first half of the thirteenth century, although it is possible that more extensive excavation in and around the church when it was excavated in 1976 might have revealed traces of an earlier church building.

In the first half of the thirteenth century Chichester was a flourishing market town and port. The area in which the new church of St. Andrew was built was the business and trading centre of the city. The density of population can be gauged from the number of what now seem uneconomically small parishes which existed in this quadrant of the city – St. Peter, North Street, Little St. Peter's at Greyfriar's Gate, St. Olave, St. Martin and St. Andrew itself. The busy life of the city was carried on all around the new church. The cattle market was held in East Street and probably extended up Cow Lane, a lane now lost, which led north from East Street just to the East of the church. This lane was suffering from encroachments as early as 1491, and disappeared completely at a very early date. It met East Street probably at the point where no. 29 now stands. The proximity of St. Andrew's church to the cattle market gave it the name of St. Andrew Oxmarket, to distinguish it from the now-vanished church of St. Andrew in the Pallant. To the north and west of the church there would be the overflow from the pig market held in St. Martin's Lane.

The new church was of very simple design and construction, but was quite adequately endowed. For Pope Nicholas's Taxation in 1291, of the city churches only St. Peter the Great and St. Pancras were taxed. However, at the same period, for the payment of Peter's Pence St. Andrew's was assessed at 4¾d., which was considerably more than any other city church except St. Peter the Great, which was assessed at 8d. The annual value of the living was given in 1521 as £6. By 1617, the church's glebe consisted of only 2 acres, one of which a parishioner, Thomas Greenfield, was keeping in his own hands. The then rector's wife, Mary Lilliat, taught children to sew in order to augment her husband's income.

According to the glebe terrier made in 1635/6, the rector of St. Andrew's was entitled to a yearly tithe of 4s. 4d. from every house worth over 20s. rent, and 2s. 2d. from every house worth under 20s. rent. The terrier did not say how much this yielded, but it would seem that few rectors ever found the stipend sufficient to live on. Many of the rectors held the living in plurality, with another of the churches in or near the city, or with one of the offices in the Cathedral establishment.

The earliest episcopal visitation of the parish for which records survive was held in 1397. At a visitation, the incumbent and leading parishioners had to appear before the bishop or his official, to report on the state of the parish and the church. In 1397 John Skyrell, the rector, appeared with Henry Prickelove, William Isaac senior and John Cruk, three of his parishioners. They all presented that all was well in the parish, and the entry in the register says no more. Already by this date, the Rectory of St. Andrew's was held by a member of the Cathedral establishment, as it was to be so often. John Skyrell was a Vicar Choral, as were John Horsham, Rector at the 1441 visitation, and Humfrey Taylor, who appeared as Rector at the 1521 visitation.

At the visitation, as has been said, the leading parishioners or churchwardens were supposed to present any faults or deficiencies in the running of the parish, the upkeep of the church or the lives of the parishioners. They were also obliged to present these at least once a year to the ecclesiastical court. It was the custom in Chichester diocese to present twice a year, at Easter and Michaelmas, as well as at any visitation. The ecclesiastical court to which the churchwardens of Chichester parishes presented was the Dean's Court, as Chichester was under his jurisdiction. Unfortunately records of this court survive only from the late sixteenth century, and by the late seventeenth century they have become very abbreviated and formal. However for the period for which they do survive, the records of the Dean's Court cast an interesting light on the daily life of the parish. It must, however, be born in mind that they only record the misdemeanours of parish officers and inhabitants, and that countless people who never incurred the wrath of the church courts went unrecorded.

In St. Andrew's parish, one of the most frequent problems in the running of the church was the acquisition of the correct texts, which were prescribed by law. In 1579 the churchwardens presented that they had no Book of Homilies, and no Paraphrases of Erasmus, both of which every church was supposed to have. The churchwardens were ordered to purchase copies, but it seems that they did not do as they were ordered. In 1582, 1589 and again in 1600, they presented exactly the same. It was not until 1639 that a Book of Homilies was finally bought for the church.

Bad behaviour on the part of the parishioners was something which the churchwardens had frequently to present. Brawls in the churchyard were quite common, and parishioners even came to blows within the church itself. In January 1583 Edward Nele was presented for "disquieting and brawling in church at

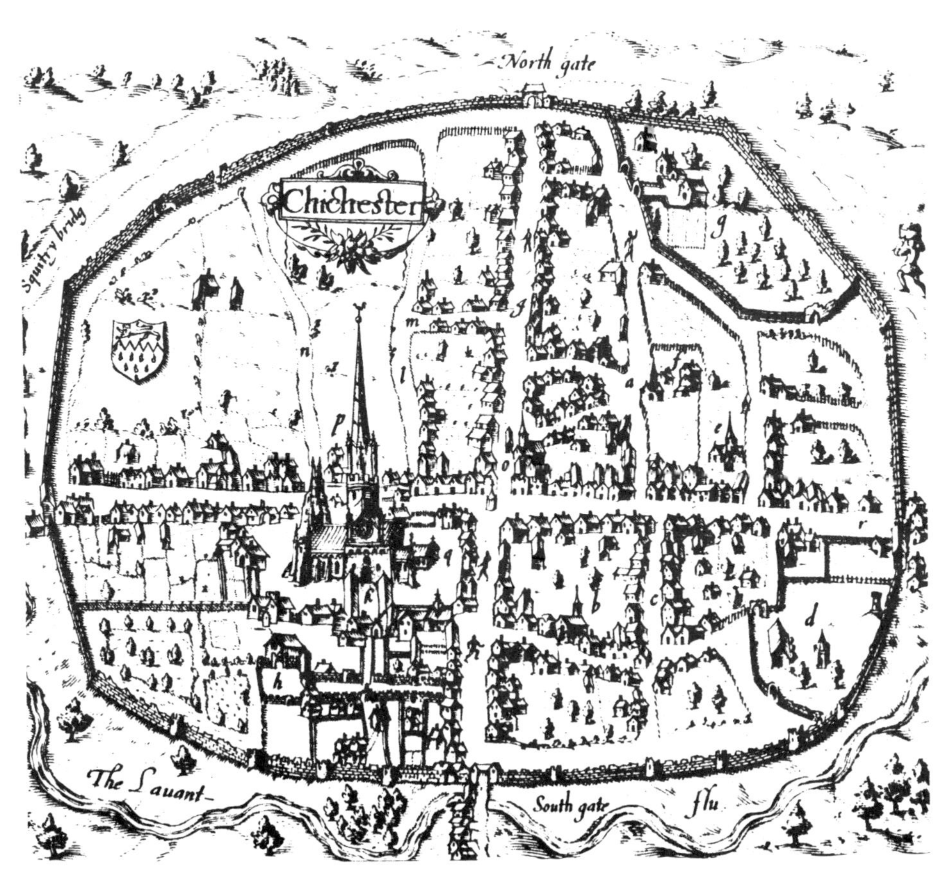

Chichester in 1595, with St. Andrew's Church marked 'e'

service time". Nele said in his defence that he did have an argument with Anthony Buttery, the then incumbent, but submitted that it took place after the service was over. Certainly the incident did not bring any disgrace on him, for later in the same year he was elected churchwarden.

In December 1600, George and Richard Arderne had an argument with Thomas Bower in the churchyard, and "strooke up" his heels, that is, tripped him up. Daggers were drawn on both sides, although Thomas Bower said in his defence that "he did drawe his dagger but not with intent to strike". All three parties were admonished by the judge before being dismissed. In July 1605 John Smith was prosecuted for striking and beating Thomas Heberden in the church "and throwing him over the bier and so hurting his face and Making it bleed".

It was not only bad behaviour in the church and its precincts which concerned the churchwardens. All aspects of the moral life of the parishioners came within the purview of the church courts. Thus, in January 1584, Alice, wife of John Osborne, was presented as being "a slanderous woman with her tongue and an unquiet woman among her neighbours". In 1585 Randall Barber was presented as a common drunkard and blasphemer, and William Rutter for bigamy. In March 1587 Thomas and Joan Roffe were accused of being slanderers of their neighbours, sowers of discord and common drunkards, who would not pay their money due to the fund for church repairs. In the same month, William Coombs was presented for lewd behaviour in Little London with one Stoke's wife.

In September 1603 Randall Barber was in trouble again, because he had been "very drunk and in his drunkeness misused Mr. Adames and other his neighbours with most bad and vilde speeches". In spite of their clashes with the ecclesiastical authorities, in 1592, Randall Barber and Thomas Roffe were the churchwardens, and were themselves presenting their fellow parishioners' misdemeanours. It must be noted that St. Andrew's parish was neither better nor worse than any other parish in the city in such matters. Presentments for, among other things, drunkeness, immorality, blasphemy, gaming and for abusive language, and for minor acts of violence were made by the churchwardens of all the parishes in Chichester at this period.

The incumbents themselves did not always meet with the churchwardens' approval. In 1605 Constantine Turton, the curate, was serving another cure as well as St. Andrew's, and had not any time to instruct the young people of his own parish in their catechism, as he should have done. In 1609 John Meade, curate and sequestrator, was also reported for not catechising the young, and for omitting to say services. By 1614 he had evidently not mended his ways. He was at the time rector of Racton, and this interfered with his duties in St. Andrew's parish. The churchwardens said that "being no preacher he doth not procure any other to preach for him neither dothe he read any homilies and upon Wednesdays and Fridays he doth not read service at all he doth alsoe neglect to instruct the youth according to the Article at any time. We have had no communion in our parish since the Thursday after Easter last . . . ."

John Meade was obviously inefficient in many ways. The parish registers were so ill-kept in 1613 that the churchwarden, Nicholas Wilde, was quite unable to send a transcript of them to the Bishop, as he was required by law to do. On 28 September 1614, Meade was ordered by the church court to produce the papers appointing him sequestrator and curate of the parish, and not to serve the cure until he had done so. He was also ordered to produce a full account of all the income he had received while incumbent. It seems as though some doubt had been cast upon his appointment to the living, which he had held for four years. Certainly, on 30 September, John Lilliot was appointed sequestrator and curate in his place.

The fabric of the church and the condition of the churchyard were of constant concern to the churchwardens at this period. It was the duty of the rector to pay for the upkeep of the chancel, while the parishioners paid for the upkeep of the rest of the church and the churchyard. Often the parishioners were loth to pay their dues towards the repair of the church, and, as a result, it seems that repairs were often botched up, and the building was often in bad repair again before very long.

In March 1603/4 Richard Michell and Robert Jenman, churchwardens, described the condition of the church in the following terms : "The particion is verie fowle and ruinous, the pavings are decayed the seates are verie badd and all unborded the walles be very fowle the font is much decayed the communion table hath verie badd furniture ther is no sentences written on the walles the doore at the west ende of the churche is verie rooton the west ende of the churche lyeth verie undecenlie within the churche porche is reddie to fall downe".

The condition of St. Andrew's church was no worse than that of the other Chichester churches, and was even better than some. At one time, the parishioners in another of the little churches could not use many of the seats in their church because the roof was unsafe and leaked in many places. The churchwardens of St. Andrew's acted with great efficiency in getting the church repaired. Quite soon after the original presentment, probably in 1604, the same churchwardens presented "that our churche is newlie Repayred and amended and was by ester last as well in pavinge the Seates with Bricke and mending the Seates and the paments under foote, in white lyminge and wasshinge the same and in makinge of a newe doore att the west end of the said churche. Also the tenn Commandements and other Sentences of holie scritures are writen about the same churche". This description gives one some idea of how the interior of the church looked at the beginning of the seventeenth century, with its white-washed walls ornamented with the ten commandments and scriptural quotations.

All was still not well with the church fabric. At the same time that they reported on the renovation of the main part of the church, the churchwardens reported that "oure vestere is greatly in Rewyn and dikeye but who shold amend the same we know not". This entry cast some doubt on the veracity of the previous churchwardens, who, as recently as October 1603, had presented "that the vestrye adjioyning to the churche is well repaired".

The state of the churchyard was also causing concern at this time. The responsibility for fencing the churchyard was divided among certain of the parishioners. Each was responsible for the upkeep of one or more 'panel' of the fence. That they often neglected their responsibility in this is obvious from the court records. In 1592, 1607, 1609 and again in 1612, 1616 and 1628, they contain references to the churchyard fence being in a state of neglect and decay. In 1631, however, the churchwardens proudly presented that "our churchyard is kept sweet and clean".

One of the recurrent dangers facing the inhabitants of Chichester in the 16th and 17th centuries was the plague. The plague of 1563 seems from surviving records to have killed about one quarter of the city's population. Unfortunately there is no record of its impact on St. Andrew's parish. In 1607 the plague again came to Chichester. It swept through the city increasing the death rate to three times the normal level. St. Andrew's parish seems to have been affected earlier than most of the city, for in 1607 the number of deaths registered soared to twenty four, from one in the previous year. From the figures taken from the parish registers which survive, it would seem that the plague came into All Saints in the Pallant and St. Andrew's parish in 1607, and spread to the rest of the city in 1608.

In 1608 the number of burials in St. Andrew's parish shot up again, to thirty six. The majority of the deaths occurred from July to October, when the plague was obviously at its height. Indeed the situation within the city was so grave that the September Quarter Sessions for that year were prorogued until 1609. In St. Andrew's parish itself the situation became so bad that the church was closed down for five and a half months in the latter half of 1608. In March 1609 the churchwardens complained to the Dean's Court that Constantine Turton, then curate, did not preach sermons, nor procure anyone else to preach them. They also complained that he had said no service at all for twenty two weeks.

Turton's defence was that he had procured four sermons a year, which was all the church law required. As for the twenty two weeks lapse, "it was in the tyme of thinfection, and therefore did forbere to say service with the consent of the church wardens and other parishioners of the better sorte". In spite of this excuse, the Dean's Commissary, who was presiding over the court, evidently decided that Turton was not fulfilling his duties as curate. He was forbidden to continue as curate of the parish, and was in fact replaced by John Meade, who, as has been mentioned, did not prove very satisfactory either.

Not all the inhabitants of the parish in the late sixteenth and seventeenth centuries were prepared to conform to the established church. There was a large and close-knit community in Chichester which remained loyal to the Catholic faith. One of the leading families in this community was the Bullaker family, of whom William lived for a time in St. Andrew's parish. William Bullaker was a noted grammarian and phoneticist, and the author of the first English grammar. He was educated in Petworth and served in the campaigns in France in 1557 and 1558. He came to Chichester and in 1571 married Elizabeth Diggons, daughter of a former mayor of the city. The couple had become parishioners of St. Andrew's by 1573, when their second child was baptised there.

William Bullaker seems to have stayed out of real trouble with the ecclesiastical authorities because of his Catholic recusancy until the end of the sixteenth century. He was churchwarden of St. Andrew's from 1576 to1579, during which time he was presented to the court with his wife for not receiving communion. Indeed in 1575 he had been excommunicated. In 1582 he was presented for teaching without a licence, but was immediately granted one. Both William and his wife were among the victims of the 1608 plague.

It would seem that in the late sixteenth century St. Andrew's was a parish in which those who did not entirely conform to the established church could live in comparative safety. This seems to have ended in 1601 when eleven people were presented for not receiving communion, as opposed to three in 1591. After 1601 the only "absolute recusant" presented to the authorities by St. Andrew's parish was Joan Ipsley *alias* Millington. Even she did not seem to have suffered much persecution, and it was often her husband Thomas, as churchwarden, who presented her.

From the early years of the seventeenth century on, Puritan non-conformity rather than Catholic was the growing problem. In Chichester in the 1630's, those with Puritan inclinations went to St. Pancras church, regardless of their parish, where William Speed, the rector, held services which were presumably more to their liking. Indeed matters came to such a state that not only were the absent Puritans presented by their own parishes for not attending the proper church, but the parishioners of St. Pancras complained to the Dean's Court that they could not even find standing room, let alone their own seats, in their church because of the press of strangers. A gallery was erected to provide seats for the strangers, but at the Archbishop's visitation in 1635, Mr. Speed had to promise to take it down again, and "confessed his error in being too popular in the pulpit".

In 1635, probably in connection with Archbishop Laud's visitation, the Dean of Chichester issued injunctions to all the curates of the city churches. These were part of a nationwide attempt to improve the standard of pastoral care and ensure observance of the rituals of the established church. One of the major concerns was the proper catechising of children, and the curates were enjoined to ask every householder for the names of all their children and servants to ensure that no one was missing their instruction in the catechism.

The curates were also enjoined to wear the surplice and the hood appropriate to their degree whenever they read prayers. The injunctions were evidently followed up, for in 1638 Durrant Hunt, then rector of St. Andrew's and Vicar Choral, was summoned before the Dean's Court with two other Vicars Choral for not wearing a surplice when saying prayers in the Subdeanery Church in the Cathedral, and for not including certain canticles in their correct places in the service.

The attempts to impose uniformity and to raise the standards of the established church came to an end in the chaos of the Civil War. St. Andrew's parish did not suffer anything like the devastation inflicted on the neighbouring parish of St. Pancras during the siege of Chichester. It would seem from the surviving accounts of the overseers of the poor, that the disturbances had little effect on the daily life of the parish. Certainly there is no dramatic increase in the Civil War period in the amount of money spent on the upkeep of the poor of the parish. There is a steady rise in the amount, but this probably reflects the economic effects of the war throughout the country.

However, between 1649/50, when all ecclesiastical property was surveyed on behalf of its new owner, Parliament, and 1656, the value of the living of St. Andrews dropped from £9 to £5. The large Subdeanery parish suffered a similar drop in value from £50 to £24, although St. Olave's lost only £1 in value and St. Martin's stayed the same. The loss in the Subdeanery parish is perhaps partly explicable by the abolition of the Cathedral establishment, which would have resulted in the impoverishment or removal from the city of many people who held houses in the parish. The drop in value of St. Andrew's parish is not however similarly explicable.

As part of Cromwell's rationalisation of the livings of the church, the whole of Chichester was to be divided into two parishes only. One of these was to be centred on St. Andrew's, and was to include the former parishes of St. Peter, North Street, St. Pancras and St. Martin's as well as St. Andrew's itself. In 1656 the new enlarged parish of St. Andrew's was established. Durrant Hunt, who was still rector in 1649/50, having been ejected in 1657, William Martyn was instituted to the new enlarged living. It is difficult to establish how far the reorganisation was actually put into effect. Certainly St. Andrew's is one of the few parishes the registers of which continue to be kept, even though they are in some confusion, throughout the Civil War and Interregnum. However, the introduction of Civil Registration in 1653 seems to have had an adverse effect on the keeping of all the registers.

At the Restoration in 1660, all the reforms of the interregnum were rescinded. Chichester was once more divided into its parishes, William Martyn was ejected from his living, and Durrant Hunt returned to St. Andrew's. He did not stay to enjoy his reinstatement for very long, for in 1662 he left to become a priest-vicar at Salisbury Cathedral.

Chichester, in the period after the Restoration was an unhappy and divided city. The suburbs outside Eastgate and Westgate had been destroyed during the siege, and buildings outside Southgate destroyed presumably as a defensive measure at some time before 1647, when Chichester was a garrison town. The Cathedral and Close had suffered considerable damage. Another epidemic of the plague is said to have hit the city in 1665, although it left no record in the register of burials for St. Andrew's parish. The restored Cathedral hierarchy was torn by faction, and matters were made worse in 1679 by the appointment of an old and irascible former Royalist soldier as bishop.

The city too had its factions, which supported their own side in the Cathedral disputes. The non-conformist faction was led by the influential Farrington family. St. Andrew's parish encompassed its own little community of non-conformists. According to the Compton Census of 1676 there were one hundred and seventeen conformist adult males in the parish, and seven non-conformists. In the 1670's men such as Joseph Postlethwaite, Thomas Booker, William Hurtson and others, refused to come to church, or to have their children baptised, and were very reluctant to pay any taxes to the church. Anthony Smyth, a reputed Quaker, presented to the church courts in 1675, never came to church and refused to pay any sort of taxes at all.

An unusually large tax assessment for the repair of the churchyard seems to have been made in March 1666, perhaps indicating that the churchyard had suffered at least neglect during the interregnum period. Thirteen people including several with known non-conformist tendencies were presented for not paying the tax. In 1668 and 1671 Abraham Haslock, then rector of St. Andrew's, brought actions in the church courts against six of his parishioners, at least two of whom were non-conformists, for keeping back tithes which they were obliged to pay to him. Many of the same names appear again in 1682 on a list of those who would not pay their tax towards the repair of the church.

The fabric of the church was as usual requiring regular attention. In 1675 the churchwardens presented that the church was in good repair, with all the necessary fittings. However, the vestry was in need of repair and no one knew who was responsible for its upkeep. Apparently no one had accepted responsibility for it since before 1604, when the current churchwardens were similarly ignorant. The churchwardens also presented that John Peachey and the Widow Carr had doorways from their houses leading directly into the churchyard, and although this should not have been allowed to happen, the churchwardens thought it "noe great annoyance".

The vestry was still in a bad state of repair in 1685. So too was part of the chancel, and the chancel windows needed reglazing. The seats in the church were also in need of repair. In their next presentment made in January 1686, the churchwardens swore that all was now well with the fabric and fittings of the church, and they did the same in 1686 and 1687. Doubts are cast on their probity, however, by the orders which the court found it necessary to give to the churchwardens in February of 1687. They were to provide communion rails for the church, and also copies of the Canons, the Thirty Nine Articles, a Table of Degrees of Marriage, and a new Common Prayer Book.

With the end of the seventeenth century the records of the church courts also come to an end, and with them any detailed information on the day-to-day life of the parish. The churchwardens' presentments from this date on are made on printed forms, and contain little information. In the more secular minded eighteenth century the church had, in any case, considerably less influence on daily life. Even the observance of Sunday as a day of rest was no longer enforceable. In 1745 the churchwardens were asked if there were any in their parish "who follow worldly employments on Sundays or frequent public houses in time of divine service". Their answer was simply "Abundance".

There must have been, however, despite the attraction of more secular activities, and the rise of the non-conformist sects, sufficient people to more than fill St. Andrew's church in the mid eighteenth century. In 1756 William Milton, the churchwarden, asked for permission to build a gallery at the west end of the church, with a staircase up to it, and a window to light it. All this he was prepared to do, and did, at his own expense. In 1755 there were one hundred and forty eight properties listed in the Poor Tax assessment for St. Andrew's, and obviously the inhabitants of these properties were more than filling the available seating accommodation.

The curate of St. Andrew's at this time was Richard Shenton, a remarkable man. As a correspondent of Thomas Wharton he would probably have known William Collins, the poet, and one of the most distinguished people connected with St. Andrew's. Shenton would almost certainly have had the duty of conducting Collins's funeral service in 1759.

Shenton was a great pluralist, holding at various times between 1752 and 1785, besides the living of St. Andrew's, those of St. Martin's and St. Bartholemew's in Chichester, Racton, West Dean, Singleton and Earnley, in addition to holding the position of Vicar Choral in the Cathedral. The tenure of these numerous livings did not make him a wealthy man. Many of them were more aptly described as starvings, and fulfilling the duties in three city parishes as well as at least three country parishes in addition to performing his duties in the Cathedral, must have made Shenton's life an extremely busy one. He found time however to sing in subscription concerts held in Chichester, as we know from the diary of Sylas Neville, who described such a concert which he attended in 1781. He also found time to teach singing to Eliza, the daughter of Dean Ball, later to become the first wife of William Hayley, the poet. Shenton's wife, formerly Mary Russell, ran a school with her two sisters, at which Hayley himself learned to read. Hayley composed one of his celebrated epitaphs about Shenton, singling out for particular praise his fine singing voice. Hayley wrote :—

Mild Shenton go in heavenly choirs to raise
That voice so suited to thy maker's Praise
Heaven's justly thine whose sacred notes so long
Flow'd a sweet earnest of celestial song

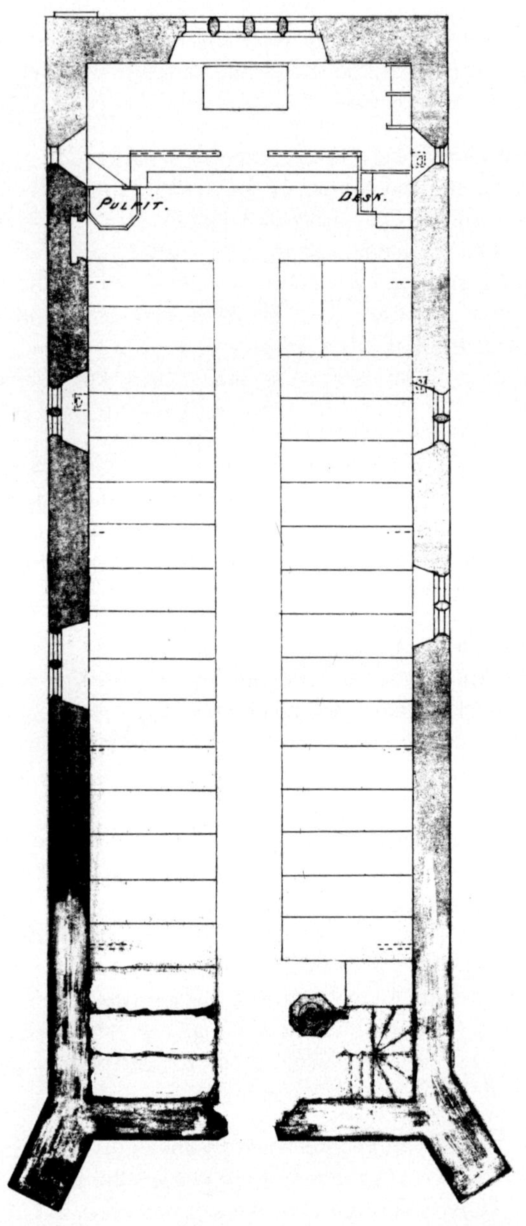

The plan of the church in the mid-nineteenth century

Yet here thy name shall live endear'd to earth
By tuneful Talents and by placid worth

During the early nineteenth century the population of St. Andrew's parish was rising quite quickly. In 1801 the total population was 573, in 1811 – 649, in 1821 – 708, and it reached its peak in 1831 when the total population rose to 719. It was estimated that only one third of the population came regularly to church, so that the seating in the church for 215 adults and about 30 children was considered adequate, at least until the middle of the nineteenth century.

The fall in church attendance to about one third of the population did bring financial problems to a small parish like St. Andrew's. In 1848 a church rate of 4d. in the pound was levied but in 1856 the vestry decided to solicit voluntary subscriptions to meet necessary parish expenses, rather than to make a church rate. In 1856, 50 people subscribed and £18. 14s. 4d. was raised. The problem with this method of voluntary contribution was that it relied heavily on the generosity of a few. In fact St. Andrew's got quite badly into debt while the voluntary subscription scheme operated, and in 1867, introduced a monthly offertory system to improve the parish finances.

If the donations to the fund for parish expenses were insufficient for its purposes the parish was always very fortunate in the nineteenth century in its appeals for funds for specific projects. In 1843, Rev. W.W. Holland donated two stained glass windows in the chancel, in memory of his mother. The windows depicted principal events in the life of St. Andrew, and were made by T. Willement of London at a total cost of £32. 18s.3d.

In 1849 a fund was set up to pay for extensive repairs to the church, and £91.17s. 0d. was raised, the subscription being led by Rev. W.W. Holland with £25. Among contributions to the fund was £16.12s. 0d. raised at a special service at which the preacher was Henry Manning, Archdeacon of Chichester, later to join the Catholic Church and become a Cardinal.

Another subscription was raised in 1855 to pay for a new organ. It was bought through Henry Bennett of South Street in Chichester, Professor of Music, and Cathedral Organist, who tested the organ, and reported on it to the vestry. The total cost, including the conveyance to Chichester, was £75, £10 of which was supplied by the sale of the old organ.

By the 1850's, the parish had become deeply divided on the question of the

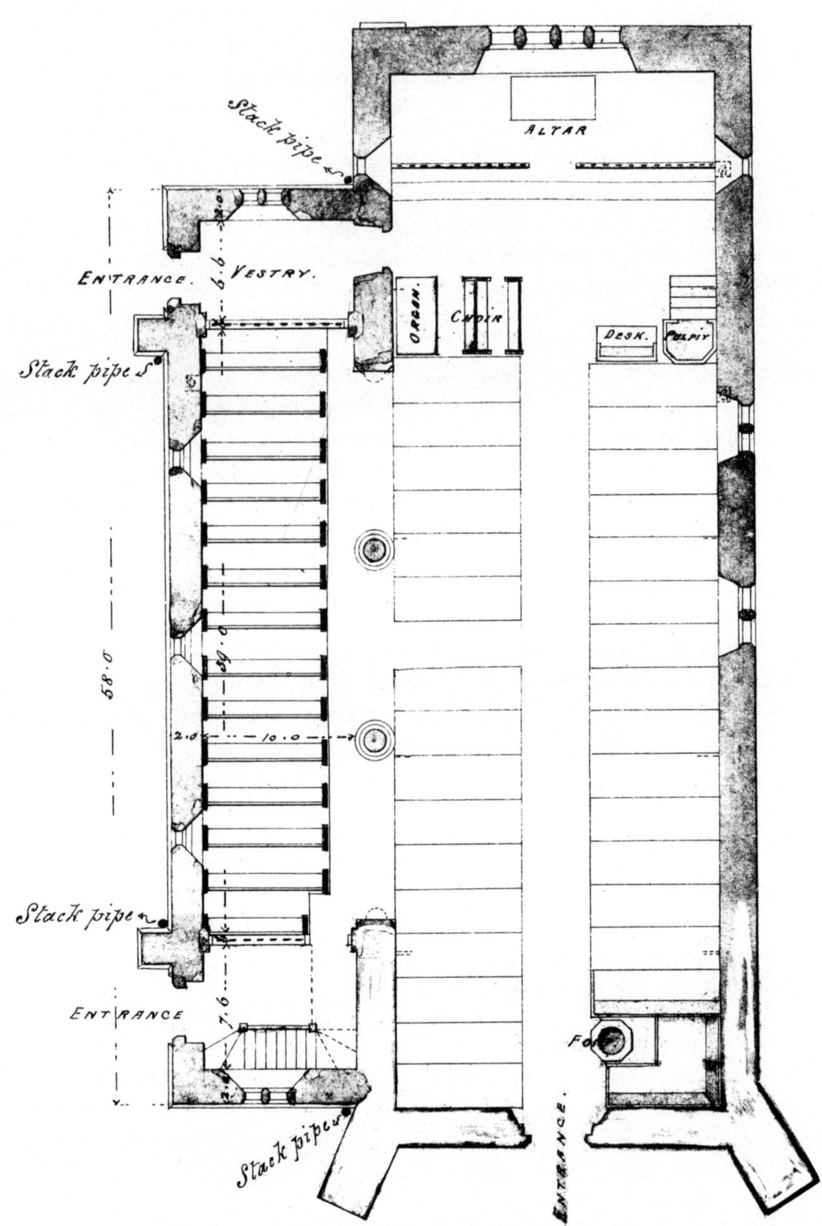

The proposed north aisle and alterations, 1856

need to enlarge the church. The rector and churchwardens, apparently on their own initiative, had plans drawn up for a new north aisle. They applied for a grant from the Incorporated Society for the Enlargement, Building and Repairing of Churches, giving as their reason, the existence of the large extra-parochial area of New Town, which adjoined St. Andrew's parish, and had no parish church.

Angry parishioners called a special vestry meeting, at which William Hayley Mason, the printer of East Street, and John Voyze Hodge, a grocer from St. Martin's, led the opposition. The parishioners were angry because they had not been consulted about the plans, even though they would presumably have been asked for subscriptions towards the new aisle once the plans had been passed. The parishioners also doubted that any more church accommodation was needed in the area. New Town was certainly an extra-parochial district but it contained the chapel of St. John, which had seating for a thousand people, including 400 free sittings and 140 open seats for domestic servants. The clerk of St. John's, Rev. Stephen Barbut, lived in St. John's Street, and had been a very faithful and hardworking minister there for forty years. He ran a very successful Sunday School, and even attracted inhabitants of St. Andrew's parish. A sizeable proportion of those attending St. Andrew's church were not, in fact, resident in the parish, and seats in the chancel had recently been let to non-parishioners at one guinea *per annum.*

The parishioners thought that for a parish of 670 people, a church with seating for 215 adults and 34 children was perfectly adequate, since the accepted church attendance rate was one third. Also any addition to the church would necessarily be built over a part of the graveyard which as parishioners said "overflows with the remains of the dead". Added to this was the fact that extensive repairs and reseating had been carried out within the last decade, the considerable expenses of which had mostly been met by subscriptions from the parishioners. They quite understandably felt that they had no wish to subscribe yet more money for the erection of a new aisle, which they considered unnecessary. The meeting, therefore, resolved by 26 votes to 6 to oppose vigorously any attempt to obtain a faculty for the erection of the new aisle.

From the plans drawn up by Thomas Rassell of Chichester for submission to the Incorporated Society, one can see both the arrangement of the existing church, in 1856, and what the rector and the churchwardens wished to add to it. In 1856 the newly acquired organ was in the centre of the gallery, the pulpit to the left of the altar, and the reading desk to the right. The plan was to bring the organ down into the body of the church, to the left of the altar, by the division between the proposed north aisle and the proposed vestry. Both pulpit and reading desk were to be placed on the right of the altar. The walls were to be of rubble faced in flint to match the existing church. Out of the 302 seats which the enlarged church would contain, 102 were to be reserved to the poor. Indeed this was a condition for receiving the £45 grant for the project from the Incorporated Society. In the face of much opposition from the parishioners, the whole project came to nothing. It would seem that St. Andrew's was considered to have a reasonable amount of accommodation since it was chosen for the holding of the Cathedral services after the fall of the Cathedral spire in February 1861.

The matter of enlarging the church was raised again ten years later in November 1866, when a special vestry was again called to discuss the question. In spite of attempts by the churchwardens to redistribute the seats many people were still dissatisfied with the provision of seating accommodation. It was claimed that several tradesmen had no seats at all, or had only half a pew, which they considered inadequate for their requirements. As a result, some tradesmen no longer attended church. Among the poorer people matters were even worse, and there were 57 households of the poor for which there was no seating accommodation at all. Very few of them ever came to church. A few seats were always free during service time, but people were unwilling to take spare seats, preferring to have a permanent seat of their own.

In spite of the strong arguments put forward, the motion to extend the church was overwhelmingly defeated by 29 votes to 5. It was, however, decided to undertake certain repairs and renovations in the church. In late 1866 a tender was accepted from F.M. Vick for washing, repairing and twice colouring the whole of the walls, ceiling and gallery. All the tablets and tables in the church were cleaned, the floor repaired and the seats under the gallery refixed. The total cost of this was estimated at £9.10s.0d.

The cleaning and renovation work continued into 1867. A special fund was set up in April 1867 for the repair of the church and the erecting of a vestry. A total of £158.13s.0d. was collected. James Rodgers, the plumber, was responsible for repairing and cleaning the windows, including the chancel window, which had been broken when a tree in the churchyard was felled. He also stripped and re-painted all the doors and irongates in and around the church.

F.M. Vick's estimate for building the vestry and for alterations within the church in connection with this was £49.12s.6d. In addition to building and glazing the vestry, he was to put in a stone arch for the organ which was to be brought down from the gallery, and rearrange the seats around it. The seats in the gallery where the organ had been were also to be made good.

The new vestry was to be reached through the doorway, then blocked with rubble, which had originally led to the old vestry, which had been in disrepair in 1685 and had presumably fallen down at some time in the eighteenth or early nineteenth century. The rubble was to be removed from the doorway and a new door provided.

Over £67 was spent on minor repairs and new fittings for the church in 1867, in addition to the erection of the new vestry. Indeed, in the late 1860's the parish seems to have been revitalised, probably through the influence of Rev. Gregory Pennethorne, who became sequestrator in 1861 and rector in 1869. He was also Vice-Principal of the Theological College and wrote books on various church matters. Rev. Pennethorne seems to have been the first incumbent to make a definite effort to improve the lot of his poorer parishioners and to involve them in the life of the parish. It may be however that he is merely the first philanthropic rector of whose activities a record survives. What is certain is that in about 1862 Mr. Pennethorne established, almost entirely at his own expense, a parish library, which by 1869 contained 250 books. In January 1869 he started a reading class at the Rectory on Tuesday evenings, for any of his parishioners who were unable to read. He also held a musical class at the Rectory on Friday evenings.

The parish Sunday School was attracting about fifty children each week, and had considerable problems with accommodation. The school had originally met in the church, and was discontinued when it became impossible for it to meet there. Mr. Pennethorne restarted the school in a house which he hired in Little London, but this proved far too expensive. Instead, a room was hired for Sundays only, but since it was only large enough to accommodate the boys, the girls held their Sunday School at the Rectory. The boys then met for a while in the Litten schoolroom, but by June 1869 both the boys' and the girls' Sunday Schools were meeting in the Rectory, even though there was not really enough room there. The school was also very short of teachers. In connection with the Sunday School, Mr. Pennethorne founded a Boot and Shoe Club. Every child who attended Sunday School would pay in a regular weekly subscription. After a certain time of regular attendance, a bonus was added by the Club to the amount saved, and the money went towards providing footwear for the child concerned.

It was Mr. Pennethorne who rescued the parish from the parlous financial straits into which it had sunk, through the failure of its voluntary subscription system. In about 1867 he established a monthly offertory system, which greatly improved the finances of the church, although it did not succeed in bringing the church's account permanently into credit. Also in Mr. Pennethorne's time a fund was started to purchase a new organ. The one bought in 1855 had been very unsatisfactory, and the new appeal was very well received. In August 1869 the new organ, with 268 pipes, was installed.

The churchyard was by this time closed, and in July 1869 the rector gave the inhabitants of houses contiguous to it permission to make gardens there. This must have improved the appearance of the area around the church. Another improvement was effected by the closure in December 1869 of a public house which used to abut on the churchyard. The Chichester Parish Magazine for December 1869 expressed relief that the public house was now finally closed, since its patrons had on occasions desecrated not merely the churchyard, but the church itself. The public house in question was probably the *Red White and Blue,* at what is now No. 23 East Street. Its customers were so rowdy, both on and off the premises, that in January of 1861 nearby residents and tradesmen complained to Quarter Sessions that it was becoming impossible to live there. The Superintendent of Police was ordered to call on Edward Combs the landlord, and warn him that the riotous behaviour must cease, but the warning apparently had little effect.

In May of 1870, one of the oldest inhabitants of St. Andrew's gave up his formal connection with the church. Mr. Glover had been parish clerk for 50 years, and was then nearly 90 years of age. A collection was raised for him and he was presented with a purse containing over £30, a considerable amount of money at the time, by a grateful parish. Also in 1870 Rev. Pennethorne left St. Andrew's parish to become vicar of Ferring with Kingston and East Preston. His place was taken by Canon A.R. Ashwell, who was also Principal of the Theological College. During his time St. Andrew's acquired a Parochial Room in Little London in which to hold its various meetings. The room was completely refitted and refurnished. The Sunday School met there every Sunday at 2.00 p.m. The Mothers Meeting was held there every Friday from 2.00 p.m. to 4.00 p.m. In February of 1872 a night school was started in the Parish Room. It was run by Rev. A.H. Smith, who was Curate of St. Andrew's, assisted by the Reader Mr. Botry Pigott, and Mr. Page, a student from the Theological College. Average attendance in the early weeks was 8, and this was gradually increasing. By December 1872 the night school for boys was held on Tuesdays and Thursdays, the similar school for girls on Mondays and Fridays.

During this time extensive work was going on in the church. The church was closed from 5 May to 23 June because of the renovations, and the services were held at St. John's. When the church was reopened the work was still not completed; the chancel had not been refitted, and the chancel walls were still in need of repair. In the autumn of 1876 the vestry decided to start a fund for certain major alterations to the church. In December a faculty was applied for to erect a stained glass window at the east end of the church, to alter or remove all the old box pews, and to install heating in or under the church, provided it could be done without disturbing any vaults. The faculty itself cost the parish £8. 4s. 10d. in fees, and a special effort was obviously necessary in order to meet the cost of the whole venture.

In order to attract donations, the organisers of the appeal asked people to contribute towards the cost of one of the three lights of the window. The rector, Rev. James Fraser, and his friends promised to pay for the right hand light. Other subscribers included Mrs. Dunford, wife of the Bishop of Chichester, Dean Burgon, the Dean of Chichester, Canon Swainson and Canon Walker, two of the residentiaries, and Canon Ashwell, the former rector of St. Andrew's, The stained glass window was made by Messrs. Frampton and Hean of the Strand, London. It cost £125. The fund was opened in October of 1876, and by Christmas had passed £100. By the time the bill was received from Messrs. Frampton and Hean at the end of April 1877, over £150 had been raised. The final total raised was £169. 18s. 1d., of which the Rector personally had donated £26. 7s. 0d.

The accounts of the parish for 1879 – 80 show the parish finances in a reasonably healthy state. All money collected at the 8 a.m. Communion was put into a fund to buy hymn books and books for confirmation candidates. Now that the parish had its own Parish Room, it was able to let it out during the week to the ' Good Templars ', which provided the parish with a small regular income. The parish had sufficient surplus to run a 'Sick and Needy' fund, with which they purchased groceries, meat, coal and Christmas presents for those members of the parish in distress. The only large expenditure at this time was on the renewal of the church path. It cost only £17. 18s. 10d., but the parish did not pay off the debt in full until 1883.

The services at St. Andrew's in this period were as follows : 7 p.m. Evensong, litany and sermon on the 1st and 3rd Sundays, 8 a.m. Holy Communion and 7 p.m. Evensong and sermon on the 2nd and 4th Sundays. From October 1878 until 1879 the living was in sequestration, and united to that of All Saints. A variety of clerics were paid £1. 1s. 0d. for each service which they conducted. In 1879 the Rev. T. Daniel Hopkyns was made rector of St. Andrew's with All Saints. He obviously did not find the combined income from both parishes sufficient to live on. In the printed accounts for 1886 – 1887, he pointed out to the parishioners that his entire income, including all his fees and offertories was only £195, and neither of the livings had a parsonage house to go with it. He exhorted them to give more generously to his offertory. His complaint seems to have had some effect, for the total of his income for the next year rose to £211.14s.3d.

Not all the offertory went to the rector of course. In 1889 some was put towards the church railing account to pay for new railings put up by J.O. Holt of Westgate, builder. The railings cost £32. 12s.0d., towards which the parishioners once more gave donations. The church had many small expenses at the end of the nineteenth century and the beginning of the twentieth century. In 1891 the gallery needed repair. In 1893 the church path, which had only been renewed a decade before, had to be re-layed at a cost of £10. 8s.0d. A new vestry fund was started in 1895; a fund for the repainting of the church in 1901 – 2. The hassocks needed renewing in 1903, and 14 dozen were bought for £11.18s. 5d. Eighteen new surplices for the choir cost the parish £7.8s.0d. in 1903.

An inventory, made at about the turn of the century, lists all the moveable property of St. Andrew's church. This includes an eight-day clock, presumably that given by an anonymous donor in 1872. The church also possessed two candle sticks, one cross, one desk and two vases, all in brass, for the altar. The chalice, paten and flagon were probably those described in the **Victoria County History of Sussex** (Vol. 3, p. 161), the chalice being inscribed with the date 1752, and the paton and flagon both bearing the hall-mark for 1842. In addition the church had a lectern and credence table, a prayer desk, 150 kneelers and various tables and chairs.

In 1908 the parish turned its attention to raising money for the repair of the church spire. Collections were made and donations solicited, but the parish also tried new methods of fund-raising. On 14 May 1908, a Concert was held in the Institute Hall. According to the newspaper report it was not very well attended, but was greatly enjoyed by those who did go. The entertainment was provided by an orchestra of 22 instrumentalists and a choir of 26, together with various local soloists. Miss O. Pillow, whose family kept a music shop on the corner of East and South streets, gave piano solos. A Mr. Willcocks rendered "Come into the garden Maud", and Miss A. Birkett, presumably a relative of the rector, Rev. F.J. Birkett, performed a Welsh Dance and an Irish Jig "in a charming and graceful manner". "The beautiful land of Nod" performed by Miss K. St. Clair with violin obligato by Mr. Swansborough was heartily encored. The entertainment also included humorous songs, duets, recitations and partsongs. The whole concert was organised by Mr. W.H. Rands, a hairdresser whose establishment was on the site now number 75 East Street, and Mr. R.W. Swansborough, who was organist at St. Andrew's. The concert raised £4 for the fund, a rather disappointing amount in view of the great effort put into the concert.

A jumble sale was also held by the parish, and collections were made, and by October 1909 sufficient money had been raised to allow the work to go ahead. The spire was stripped and entirely reshingled at a cost of £35. 17s. 8d.

Throughout the period of the Great War, the fabric of the church seems to have been kept in good repair. At the Archdeacon's visitation in 1921, it was reported that the fabric was in good condition, except for the plaster on the outside of the east wall. The graveyard, however, which had been closed since 1854, was full of rubbish, which the Archdeacon ordered to be cleared.

In 1927 a similar good report was given on the fabric, but by 1935 a fund was being set up for a number of minor repairs to the church. It raised £36. 14s. 9d., but the records do not reveal exactly how it was spent. In 1937 Canon Arthur Young gave the church a set of Lent altar fittings in memory of his wife. As late as 1938 a Mrs. Wingham presented an oak altar rail in memory of her father J.W. Moore, and her husband, P. Wingham, both past churchwardens of the parish, and both of course connected with the printing firm that is now Messrs. Moore and Tillyer's.

It is sad that the church should have received such gifts so shortly before it was finally closed as a place of worship. On the 10th of February, 1943, St. Andrew's church was badly damaged by a bomb. The congregation was moved to All Saints, and St. Andrew's was never used for a church service again. When Archdeacon Mason visited the church in 1948 he found that much of the plaster was down from the roof, and the windows were in a very bad state. The churchyard was neglected, and builders working nearby had caused considerable damage to it.

The benefice of St. Andrew's was united to those of St. Olave with St. Martin, St. Peter the Less, All Saints and St. Peter the Great in 1953, to form the single parish of St. Peter the Great. This meant that the church was redundant. In 1959 the organ was transferred to St. Mary's church, Rumboldswhyke, where it was very unfortunately burnt in a fire in 1960. The faculty for the disposal of the furnishings of St. Andrew's mentions the intention of turning the building into a church hall. Nothing seems to have come of this, and St. Andrew's was neglected and abandoned for many years. In 1969 the area around the church was paved, under an agreement with the City Council to create access roads to the backs of the properties in East Street. The gravestones were removed, the surface levelled off, and the gravestones were then reversed and used as paving stones.

The idea of establishing some sort of Arts Centre in St. Andrew's was first mooted in the late 1960's. It was not however until the setting up of a committee and the appointment of trustees in 1972 that the project really got under way. By January 1976 sufficient money had been raised for a start to be made on the restoration of the then sadly dilapidated church. A limited archaeological excavation was carried out within the walls of the church before a new floor was laid. The roof and walls were made sound, the windows reglazed, and the interior redecorated. In June 1976 St. Andrew's was reopened as the Chichester Centre of Arts.